HEAVEN AT ALL COST

MIKE CHUKS NWANEGBO

DEDICATION

This book is dedicated to all those who aspire to make heaven at all cost through the right route.

It is also dedicated to the brave men and women who had put their lives on the line in mission fields unlocking the gates of heaven for souls to gain access through the preaching of the gospel.

You are all indeed God's fellow workmen. You shall all shine like stars.

I want to appreciate my wife and children for going into the mission field with me. You too will shine like stars.

TABLE OF CONTENTS

INTRODUCTION

I am always moved by the emptiness I sense in people as I interact with them in society. Several people seem lost. There is so much hustle and bustle. People desperately seeking material success at all cost. They cheat, sweat, kill and do all sort of things to achieve what they call success. The word "making it" is in the mouth of every one. The question is: what is "making it"? Some achieve so much fame and financial riches yet they seem the most miserable in life. After acquiring so much wealth, some just commit suicide after discovering that it is all vanity upon vanity.

So many want to make it to a place of material success but very few ever think of making it after life on earth. So many do not care about the life after here, but the truth is that it cannot be ignored. If you ignore it, it will not ignore you. Life on earth is like a drop on the ocean compared to life after death. Life after death is for ever and cannot change.

I hear of people preparing for retirement but very few are preparing for eternal retirement. The present illusion of life and ignorance of life after death has been deepened by some invisible hands to bring men to a place of eternal regret and shame.

In the western world the need for heaven is no longer an issue. It has been relegated to the background. This is a great injustice to our generation. So many people do not have a clue of life after death, not to talk of how to get there and how to secure their future in eternity.

In this book I have tried to the best of my ability to explain the need to prepare for heaven and how to prepare and get to heaven.

I believe that by the time you are done with reading this book, your mind will be repositioned and you will no longer be afraid of death, but look to death as a transition to a better future in eternity.

4

It will also take you away from chasing the shadow of material wealth to building treasures in heaven for your eternal retirement.

If you buy into this reality, you will pursue heaven at all cost. It will become the ultimate and will change your perception of life on earth. One thing it will teach you is that there is nothing earthly worth dying for.

It will liberate you from the illusion of making money at all cost thereby releasing you to the real life on earth and a hope of eternal life in heaven

HEAVEN AT ALL COST

Every human, who is truthful to self would agree that somewhere in his or her heart, is this desire for eternity. Eternity is in all our hearts. Atheists try to suppress this natural urge for life in eternity but the truth is that it cannot be suppressed.

This hidden desire to make heaven or urge to merge with God as some would call it, has led men into desperate search for the best way to attain peaceful eternity. Some have resorted to meditation, astral travel, penance, self-mutilation etc. Some have gone to the extent of trying to please God through martyrdom. Martyrdom has been defined differently by different people. Some religions believe that killing infidels would guarantee them a place in heaven. Some do believe that defending their faith by taking up arms would guarantee them a place in heaven. What a mystery? If men are so convinced that blowing up selves or defending their religious believe would guarantee them heaven, then this heaven must be so real and must be attained at all cost. In the days of the crusade young men flocked to join the crusade in other to defend their faith and many believed that their actions would guarantee them heaven. To most, defending the faith was not the real motive but making it to heaven.

In our present age so many young men are flocking to join militant group with the belief that they would make it to heaven if they die as martyrs. Governments had wondered what attracts so many young men to join these militant groups. The answer is simple, they are responding to the innate desire of man to find an easy way to making it to heaven. Research has proved that most people that claim to go to fight to defend their faith have little or no grasp of what their religious faith really teaches. To every human, there is that desire for heaven at all cost. Yes heaven must be attained at all cost but how?

If there is heaven, how do we really get there and who will lead us to this eternal home that all humans yearn for? Most religions believe that heaven is the abode of God and going to heaven will mean going to meet God. If heaven is the abode of God, it means that only God can truly claim to know the right way to get to heaven.

Of all the so called gurus, prophets and masters, only one claimed to be the way and that one is Jesus Christ- John 14:6. He did not only claim to be the way but the only way. Others claimed to be looking for the way or claim to know the way. How can they know the way except God reveals it to them? Is Jesus really the only way to God?

I am fully convinced that Jesus is the only way. All religions somehow claim that God is Love. If God is love, it means that the best way to get to him is through love. Of all the prophets, gurus and masters, only one truly preached undiluted love. That one was Jesus Christ. Jesus commanded us to love our enemies, love our neighbours, pray for those that persecute and use us. (Matthew 5:44). Does this not sound like real love?

He commanded us not to curse, to turn the other cheek when we are hit on one cheek, to forgive so that we would be forgiven. He is the only one who boldly said that he is one with the father and that he came from the father. (John 10:30). If he is one with the father, it means that he also is love. To crown it all he was the only one who forgave sins and the forgiven felt forgiven immediately without doubt. (John 8:11). One thing that is amazing was that even demons confessed that he is the son of God.

"When He came to the other side into the country of the Gadarenes, two men who were demon-possessed met Him as they were coming out of the tombs. They were so extremely violent that no one could pass by that way. 29 And they cried out, saying, "What business do we have with each other, Son of God? Have You come here to torment us before the time?" Matthew 8: 28-29.

"Before the time"? What time one would ask? It means that even the demons know that there is a set time and that time is the end of all men; when God will judge all. If there is judgement, then there will also be punishment and reward. The condemned are sent to hell and the acquitted are rewarded in heaven.

To crown it all, Jesus resurrected and ascended to heaven. Of all the prophets, gurus and masters ever known to mankind, no one was ever recorded as resurrecting not to talk of ascending to heaven. It is worthy to note that he first descended to hell to set the captives free before ascending.

If Jesus ascended to heaven, it means that we must look at his teachings again. Apart from urging us to follow him to heaven, he warned that those who refuse to follow him will descend to hell. He warned that hell is a terrible place and that it would be better to enter into heaven with one arm cut than enter into hell full. What Jesus was saying is simply to make sure you make heaven at all cost.

My question to you today is: will you make it to heaven? Do not be deceived by your position in the church. Being a pastor cannot save you. Being a church goer cannot save you. Being a good person is not sufficient. Your righteousness is not sufficient to save you. What you need to be sure of salvation is to accept Jesus for real, obey his word and make sure you are quick to forgive. Live your life by the word and the spirit.

<u>ALL SIGNS POINT TO THE END</u>

The ice caps are melting, species are going extinct. Two hundred species are going extinct every 24 hours. The rain forest is being designated at remarkable rates. The consequences of genetically modified food are unknown; the earth is being robbed of its resources, oceans being poisoned by pollution. There is increasing global temperature. The earth is like an aging woman, unable to replenish self. The earth has been robbed of its strength.

The scientists are aware of this so they are looking for other sources of life in the Galaxies. This will not help issues because no matter what, death awaits every living soul.

The Bible clearly point out that we are in the last days. It pointed out some signs we must watch out for. One thing is clear; these signs are here. Not only that the Bible talks about these signs, but also warns us to prepare for life after death, as the end of the world will usher us before the throne of God for judgment.

For me, the most authentic sign of the end time will be those mentioned by Jesus Christ Himself. The disciples of Jesus provoked Him to reveal to us the signs of the end time in Mathew 24:3.

" …. And what shall be the sign of thy coming and of the end of the world?"

This clearly means that the coming of Jesus Christ will really mean the end of the world. I will love to list out the signs one after the other:

1. Verse 5. Many will come claimming to be Christ.

2. Verse 6-7. There will be rumours of war and Nations shall rise against Nations, Kingdoms against Kingdoms, there shall be pestilences, famine and earthquake in diverse places.

3. Verse 9-10. Christians will be persecuted and hated of all Nations for the sake of the name of Jesus. Offence will come and they shall betray one another and shall hate one another.

4. False prophets shall rise and deceive many.

5. Iniquity will abound causing the love of many to grow cold.

6. The Gospel shall be preached in the entire world for a witness unto all Nations.

If Jesus is coming again, then where had He been if not in Heaven? He said

"I go to prepare a place for you so that where I am you will also be"

Apart from the fact that this earth will also wax old and be folded away, another reason why we must make Heaven at all cost is that; if you miss Heaven, the only place left is Hell.

Whether we believe it or not, we must find out the truth at the end of life. Anybody who has not prepared for Heaven will regret at the end of life when they will suddenly discover that they had the opportunity to make heaven but ignored this great opportunity. They would cry for another chance but unfortunately there will be no other chance. It is now on earth.

WHAT HAPPENS WHEN WE DIE?

 Some religious groups simply believe in reincarnation. Reincarnation means coming back to life after death in another form. It could be in a lower life form or a superior life depending on how you lived your previous life. Reincarnation is another way of saying there is life after death. The difference is that they believe you will come back to earth to begin another circle on earth. The Atheists say that there is no life after death. They claim that if you die, you are dead and that is it for you. It really does not make sense else there would be no need for life in the first place.

One thing is clear; every human being has eternity embedded in their hearts. Some may ignore it but at the point of death, we all have questions and many are gripped by the fear of the unknown. When this earth pass away or when we pass away from this earth, where then do we go?

As a practicing Christian, I believe there is a place called Heaven. It is a place where those who accepted the covenant of God through Christ are preserved and rewarded. Some may have a different view but I would request that you reason a little with me for now. Heaven is the abode of God. It is a place characterised by righteousness, peace and joy.

Reason here with me.

If a rapist and murderer rapes and kills innocent women and is never caught by the law, do we conclude that such a one has got away free? Common sense tells us that there is always justice. For such, where will justice be served? I am sure it must be after death.

There is heaven and there is hell. Every soul will be brought to judgement after death and those whose names are found in the book of life are sent to heaven to live in eternal bliss. Those whose names are not found in the book of life are sent to eternal punishment in hell, separated from the presence of God.

How can one get his name into the book of life? This is one of the mysteries of God. God has made this very easy by sending his son Jesus Christ to die in our place. It is a covenant. Anyone who accepts Jesus Christ as having paid for his or her sins is accepted and such a person's name is written in the book of life. It sounds so easy but that is the mystery of God. That is why it is called a free gift. The moment your name is written in the book of life, God gives you the grace to live a holy life according to his commands. If you make a mistake and sin, and if you repent, the blood of Jesus is available to wash your sins. The moment you acknowledge your sins and repent; the blood of Jesus automatically washes your sins.

If you continue to sin and refuse to turn from your sins, God will send several warnings through the word and through circumstances. If you refuse to repent and die in your sin, your name will be erased from the book of life and hell will definitely become your portion. I am not saying this to scare you but to warn you.

WHAT IS HELL?

In my search on Google, I came across a definition which makes more sense to me. It defined hell as:

"A place referred in various religions as a spiritual realm of evil and suffering, often traditionally depicted as a place of perpetual fire beneath the earth where the wicked are punished after death".

Several people have given us testimonies of the existence of Hell. They have told horrible and fear gripping stories of Hell. One thing about Hell is that it is for ever and ever.

As usual with me, I would prefer to rely on Biblical information on Hell. The Bible has proven that it has never failed in its prophecies and information. Scientists have on several occasions got their clues from the Bible. Rev 21:8 tells us that those who will have their place in Hell are:

"…the fearful, and unbelieving, and the abominable, and murderers and whoremongers, and sorcerers, idolaters, and all liars shall have their part in the lake which burneth with fire and brimstone: which is the second death."

Mathew 25:30 describes it as a place of gnashing of teeth. It is a place for unprofitable servants. I hear people say that a servant of God cannot go to Hell. The Bible says that unprofitable servants can be cast into Hell. If you are not winning souls or profiting the Kingdom of God in anyway, you stand a risk of being cast into Hell. This is not to scare you but to you wake you up.

Mathew 22:13 calls it a place of outer darkness.

Luke 16:23 calls it a place of torment. The torment in Hell cannot be compared to any Kind of torment on earth.

II Samuel 22:6 calls it a place of sorrow. No sorrow on earth can be compared to the sorrow of hell especially for those who profess to be Christians but lived in sin on earth. On getting to hell, they would find that they should have been in heaven. They will have the privilege of seeing heaven from hell. There will be great sorrow and regrets.

II Thessalonians 1:9 calls it a place of everlasting destruction.

Revelation 21:8 tells us that it is a place where men are tormented with fire and brimstone.

Mark 9:44 says that it is a place where the fire is not quench.

Revelation 14:11 says it is a place where the inhabitants are tormented day and night without rest. Anyone who receives the mark of the beast will never escape this eternal torment. Be warned. This book may fall into your hand when the Christians have raptured to be with Christ. At that time the man of sin called the anti-Christ will cause men to take his mark or be killed. It is better to die than take the mark of the beast. If you take the mark, you are damned for ever. The mark of the beast is the number 666. Those who do not have the mark of the beast cannot buy nor sell. Accept Christ today and prepare for heaven at all cost; even if it means suffering on earth. The suffering on earth cannot be compared to the glory of heaven.

Revelation 20:14 calls it a lake of fire.

Luke 16:24 calls it a place of hopelessness and thirst. There will be no water to drink to quench thirst.

One thing about Hell is that the pain never subsides and one cannot die. In Hell, One has full consciousness and memories. You will always wish you were in Heaven.

It will be worse for those who were Christians but played away their salvation.

Every day, thousands of people go to hell. Many will be shocked when they are sentenced to hell. They will just find out that they had the opportunity to avoid hell but they reasoned it off. They could not see how accepting Jesus could take them to Heaven. Some easily explain all happening scientifically. In hell, your science will be useless as you will not be able to explain scientifically what is happening to you.

Hell is not a place for any human. It was not created for human beings but for the Devil and his agents. God never wills that any man should go to hell. Man goes to hell out of his own doing by freely or willingly rejecting God's offer of salvation, which is the acceptance of Jesus as our Saviour and our Lord. Hell is definitely not an option. It must be Heaven at all cost.

We must do all we can to make it to Heaven. Hell is a no go area for any soul. You do not want to end up in hell.

This reading will testify against you on the last day if you do not do anything about your soul today.

Two main things will for sure send a person to hell. The first is the refusal to accept Jesus as Lord and saviour. God has made him Lord and saviour of all souls. Refusing him means refusing God's offer of salvation for your soul. A soul that is not redeemed by the blood cannot inherit the kingdom of God and will have its place in hell.

The second thing that can send a soul to hell is living in sin. If one is redeemed but continues to live in sin without repenting, such a soul is making mockery of the redemptive blood of Christ. Hell for sure awaits such a one.

You shall be holy for the Lord thy God is Holy.

HEAVEN.

The Bible tells us of certain people that went to Heaven, Elijah was taken to Heaven in a chariot.

Many people claim to have had Heavenly encounter. Some claim they have been to Heaven and back. This we cannot verify but we can verify the account of Apostle John the beloved. The Lord Jesus ordered him to write his account. Let us take a look at it as recorded in the book of Revelation.

Rev 4:1-11.

"After this I looked, and, behold, a door was opened in heaven: and the first voice which I heard was as it were of a trumpet talking with me; which said, Come up hither, and I will shew thee things which must be hereafter. And immediately I was in the spirit: and, behold, a throne was set in heaven, and one sat on the throne. And he that sat was to look upon like a jasper and a sardine stone: and there was a rainbow round about the throne, in sight like unto an emerald. And round about the throne were four and twenty seats: and upon the seats I saw four and twenty elders sitting, clothed in white raiment; and they had on their heads crowns of gold. And out of the throne preceded lightnings and thunderings and voices: and there were seven lamps of fire burning before the throne, which are the seven Spirits of God. And before the throne there was a sea of glass like unto crystal: and in the midst of the throne, and round about the throne, were four beasts full of eyes before and behind. And the first beast was like a lion, and the second beast like a calf, and the third beast had a face as a man, and the fourth beast was like a flying eagle. And the four beasts had each of them six wings about him; and they were full of eyes within: and they rest not day and night, saying, Holy, holy, holy, LORD God Almighty, which was, and is, and is to come. And when those beasts give glory and honour and thanks to him that sat on the throne, who liveth for ever and ever, the four and twenty elders fall down before him that sat on the throne, and worship him that liveth for ever and ever, and cast their crowns before the throne, saying, Thou art worthy, O Lord, to receive glory and honour and power: for thou hast created all things, and for thy pleasure they are and were created".

Rev 21:10-27 Description of the New Jerusalem coming down from Heaven

"And he carried me away in the spirit to a great and high mountain, and shewed me that great city, the holy Jerusalem, descending out of heaven from God, Having the glory of God: and her light was like unto a stone most precious, even like a jasper stone, clear as crystal; And had a wall great and high, and had twelve gates, and at the gates twelve angels, and names written thereon, which are the names of the twelve tribes of the children of Israel: On the east three gates; on the north three gates; on the south three gates; and on the west three gates. And the wall of the city had twelve foundations, and in them the names of the twelve apostles of the Lamb. And he that talked with me had a golden reed to measure the city, and the gates thereof, and the wall thereof. And the city lieth foursquare, and the length is as large as the breadth: and he measured the city with the reed, twelve thousand furlongs. The length and the breadth and the height of it are equal. And he measured the wall thereof, an hundred and forty and four cubits, according to the measure of a man, that is, of the angel. And the building of the wall of it was of jasper: and the city was pure gold, like unto clear glass. And the foundations of the wall of the city were garnished with all manner of precious stones. The first foundation was jasper; the second, sapphire; the third, a chalcedony; the fourth, an emerald; The fifth, sardonyx; the sixth, sardius; the seventh, chrysolyte; the eighth, beryl; the ninth, a topaz; the tenth, a chrysoprasus; the eleventh, a jacinth; the twelfth, an amethyst. And the twelve gates were twelve pearls: every several gate was of one pearl: and the street of the city was pure gold, as it were transparent glass".

Several people claim to have been to Heaven and back especially in these last days. I do not dispute their claims because God wants people to experience heaven so that they can tell others. Apostle Paul talked about a man that was caught to the third heaven.

I have proved to myself that the most reliable book about prophesy and the future is the Bible. None of its predictions have ever failed. It is too precious. For the above reasons, I will want to go back to the Bible to give us information about Heaven or what heaven looks like.

The bible tells us of three Heavens:

1   The first Heaven is what we call the sky that envelopes the earth.

2   The second Heaven is the abode of the stars, the sun and the moon. Some call it the galaxies. These are and could be visible to the human eyes through the use of telescopes.

3   The third Heaven is a place of mystery. It is the abode of God, the angels and the Christians and also righteous Jews who lived before Christ who had passed to glory. It is the location of the throne of God.

I consciously stated that it is the abode of Christians because no one can enter into Heaven without Christ. Those who made it to Heaven before Christ were allowed in based on covenant with God. In these last days, God made it clear that it is only through Jesus Christ that we can enter Heaven.

This may sound difficult for you to believe but it is the unchangeable truth and there is nothing we can do about it. If you think it is a lie and that you can enter by how good you are or by another name or through any prophet, just wait till you die then you will find out the truth.

Our present flesh and blood cannot enter Heaven. Only our spirits or the new body the Christians will put on during rapture of the saints at the trumpet sound from Heaven or after death on earth.

THE VALUE OF HEAVEN

How can we quantify the value of heaven? The truth is that nothing can be compared to it. If men knew the value and quality of Heaven, they would make heaven their primary objective in life. They will be ready to trade in everything for Heaven including their lives. It is only on earth that we have the opportunity to prepare for heaven. God has given us his Word, the Holy Spirit and the angels to help us prepare for heaven.

Some false Islamic teachers have used the value of Heaven to lure unsuspecting people to suicide bombing with the promise of virgins in Heaven. Such a teaching is a teaching that appeals to lust than to genuine quest for Heaven. I have always asked why the rich and leaders of such groups do not volunteer themselves for suicide bombing, rather they send the weak. Don't they want to go to heaven?

Heaven is of great value. It has nothing to do with flesh and blood. In Heaven, we shall be like angels. There will be no marriage in Heaven as we will all be spirits and no flesh to satisfy with lust.

"At the resurrection people will neither marry nor be given in marriage; they will be like the angels in heaven". Matthew 22:30

In Heaven, Saints have the body of the spirit. We will be like Christ. Most people spend their time on earth chasing material possessions. On their death bed, it will suddenly occur to them that they will not be going into the afterlife with their earthly possessions. Solomon came to a point that he was compelled to declare:

"I have seen all the things that are done under the sun; all of them are meaningless, a chasing after the wind". Ecclesiastics 1:14.

To be quite sure of the kingdom of Heaven, you must try to purge yourself of this worldly weight that could hold you down. Paul in the

Bible talks about weights and habits that can prevent us from entering Heaven.

Understanding the value of making Heaven at all cost will help you appreciate it. Mathew 13:44 describes the value of the Kingdom of Heaven. Jesus likened it to:

"Treasure hid in a field; which when a man had found, he hideth it and for joy thereof goeth and selleth all that he had and buy that field."

The truth of the kingdom is always hid. It can only be made known by sons of God through the preaching of the Gospel of Jesus Christ. This is made possible by the Holy Spirit enablement and revelations.

The sons of God here mean; those who have accepted Jesus Christ and become adopted by faith into the family of God. This is a great mystery that the ordinary mind cannot comprehend.

When these hidden treasures of Heaven are revealed to a person through the Gospel of Christ, it generates such joy and peace that cannot be comprehended. It is of such value that those that do understand will be ready to let go of every other earthly treasure to take hold of the treasures of Heaven both on earth and in Heaven.

Salvation is a great treasure which cannot be equated with any earthly wealth. It is of such value that the wise will be ready to give all they have to hold on to salvation. Salvation is the key, way and route to Heaven. The kingdom of Heaven is such a great treasure that all should seek.

The joy that the hope of heaven brings is so deep that even in earthly poverty; the joy will not ebb away. Even at the point of death, the inner joy remains. It is a joy like flowing river that bubbles from within.

Verse 45 went further to describe the value of the kingdom of Heaven.

"The Kingdom of Heaven is like a merchant seeking beautiful pearls, who when he had found one pearl, of great price, went and sold all he had and bought it".

In life, we all have eternity in our hearts. We are all seeking eternity. Many seek for it in different ways and through different religions. Many in the quest for the kingdom of heaven afflict themselves with different afflictions and penances in order to qualify for the kingdom of Heaven. Some believe they can attain it by turning themselves into soldiers of whatever they call God. Majority believe it can be attained through a clean life style. The kingdom of Heaven is expensive and cost greatly to attain. Therefore whoever finds it, must know that he has found treasure of more value than any treasure in human existence.

Yes the kingdom of Heaven is so costly that no man can afford to pay the price. Many are seeking it but no man can find it except one seeks for it through the right channel. Let me tell you the right channel to seek and to find the kingdom of Heaven. It is simply through Jesus Christ.

Since no human can find or can enter the kingdom of Heaven because of the huge cost, God in His mercy spoke His Word and the word became flesh and we called Him Jesus Christ according to the earlier prophecy about Him. He willingly suffered death on the cross by laying down His life as a price for us to have access to Heaven. He then made available this access to all who believe in Him by faith. It means that finding Jesus is finding the pearl of great price. Jesus is the pearl of great price.

Your willingness to give everything up for the kingdom of God is what God is looking for. Do you value Heaven more than your earthly possessions and achievements? That will go a long way to tell where your heart is. The Bible says that where a man's treasure is there his heart would be. If Heaven is your treasure or if you are building or accumulating treasures in Heaven, your heart will be there and you will want to make Heaven at all cost. If your treasure is stored on this earth, you will be afraid of death, you will never be thinking about going to Heaven. How can you go to Heaven except you die or change this physical body through rapture?

Many Christians are not looking forward to rapture. They are so earthly focused that they are void of the pleasure that those who are waiting for heaven do experience. The bible says we wait in joyful hope for the coming of our Lord and saviour Jesus Christ. The hope of heaven generates such joy that surpasses human understanding. Christians are now so comfortable on earth that they have come up with teachings on how to survive on earth. These have crept into churches and have diverted the hearts of the people from heaven; which is the ultimate. Very few churches prepare people for heaven. When you begin to talk about heaven or take measures that will focus men on making heaven, they will begin leaving the church because most of their focus is on surviving this earth. When Jesus told his thousands of followers the basic truth about eternal life; majority left him and refused to walk with him ever again. The truth he told them was:

"Unless you eat the flesh of the son of man and drink his blood, you have no life within you. Whoever eats my flesh and drinks my blood has eternal life, and I will raise that person at the last day" John 6:53-54. His flesh here means the word of God. And the blood means his life which also means his spirit. The gospel of John tells us that Christ is the word of God made flesh. (John 1:14). The bible also tells us that the life is in the blood. (Leviticus 17:11).

<u>HOW TO BUILD TREASURES IN HEAVEN</u>

I call this, preparing for retirement. It is possible to build treasures in Heaven. In fact, Jesus made mention of the need to build treasures in heaven where thieves cannot break in as opposed to building on earth where thieves can break in.

Mathew 6:19-21 *"Lay not up for yourselves treasures upon earth, where moth and rust doth corrupt, and where thieves break through and steal: But lay up for yourselves treasures in heaven, where neither moth nor rust doth corrupt, and where thieves do not break through nor steal: For where your treasure is, there will your heart be also"*

The above statement by Jesus is a clear confirmation that there is a Heaven and that it has a location. That treasure can be stored in Heaven for future use in eternity. Jesus went on to point out some features of Heaven in relation to the preservation of treasures. He made it clear that there is neither rust nor aging in Heaven and there are no thieves in Heaven. It means that whatever treasure you have stored in Heaven is safe as there are no thieves to steal them. If treasures can be stored in heaven it could imply that we would not all be equal in heaven. Start building for yourselves treasures in heaven.

THE PARABLE OF THE RICH FOOL.

This is a parable that emphasizes the need not to focus on earning riches in this world without a hope of Heaven.

Luke 12:15-21 *"And he said unto them, Take heed, and beware of covetousness: for a man's life consisteth not in the abundance of the things which he possesseth. And he spake a parable unto them, saying, The ground of a certain rich man brought forth plentifully: And he thought within himself, saying, What shall I do, because I have nowhere to bestow my fruits? And he said, This will I do: I will pull down my barns, and build greater; and there will I bestow all my fruits and my goods. And I will say to my soul, Soul, thou hast much goods laid up for many years; take thine ease, eat, drink, and be merry. But God said unto him, Thou fool, this night thy soul shall be required of thee: then whose shall those things be, which thou hast provided? So is he that layeth up treasure for himself, and is not rich toward God"*.

A proper look at the above scripture will reveal a deep mystery about life on earth without the hope of Heaven. It started by warning us of covetousness and the value of real life. Jesus emphasized that life does not consist in the abundance of the things we possess. The things we possess will someday pass away. Jesus saw life on earth as only a fraction of the real life. The real life is in eternity. On earth, most people chase after the material possessions and we often equate achievement with material possessions. What Jesus is trying to point out here is that material possessions have no eternal value. What has eternal value is your relationship with God. Though, we are made to understand that your earthly possessions can be transformed into heavenly treasures if it is used according to the orders and purposes of God.

The story of the rich fool is clear. He is called a fool because he lacked the knowledge of life in eternity and the need to build treasures for eternity. Rather he was busy building treasures on earth without converting them to Heavenly treasures. Are you a fool?

Are you spending your time on earth accumulating earthly possessions? What of Heaven? Pursue Heaven at all cost.

The scripture we read above also pointed out one fact that awaits all men. That fact is that a day must come when your soul will be required of you. One thing is sure; you cannot take your earthly possessions along with you to eternity. Why labour for that which you cannot take into eternity. This does not mean that we do not need to work hard but our focus must not be towards accumulating earthly wealth without being rich towards God.

The story of the rich young ruler clearly tells us how to build or store treasures in Heaven. Mathew 19:16-22 *"And, behold, one came and said unto him, Good Master, what good thing shall I do, that I may have eternal life? And he said unto him, Why callest thou me good? there is none good but one, that is, God: but if thou wilt enter into life, keep the commandments. He saith unto him, Which? Jesus said, Thou shalt do no murder, Thou shalt not commit adultery, Thou shalt not steal, Thou shalt not bear false witness, Honour thy father and thy mother: and, Thou shalt love thy neighbour as thyself. The young man saith unto him, All these things have I kept from my youth up: what lack I yet? Jesus said unto him, If thou wilt be perfect, go and sell that thou hast, and give to the poor, and thou shalt have treasure in heaven: and come and follow me. But when the young man heard that saying, he went away sorrowful: for he had great possessions"*.

The rich young ruler had kept the law. He was sure he was qualified for heaven by keeping the law. One thing is that he really never knew himself. He was a greedy idolater who loved his money more than the kingdom of God. He never saw it. Just entering Heaven is not all. You must also build treasures in Heaven and that is done right here on earth.

In verse 21, Jesus told the rich young man to go and sell all he had and give to the poor and then follow him in order to store treasures in Heaven.

What Jesus was trying to show the man was that his (The rich man's) heart was not right. His wealth was his hidden idol which he was not ready to trade for the kingdom of God. Jesus was pointing out that giving to the poor generate treasures in eternity. This promise of giving to the poor is only for those who have accepted Jesus as their salvation. If you are not in Christ, no amount of giving to the poor will save you.

The Bible argues this when it says that "he that gives to the poor lends to the Lord". Whatever you lend to the Lord is paid back with greater interest and other treasures deposited in your Heavenly account.

We also learn from the same passages that following Jesus is rewarded with treasures in Heaven.

Offering and giving to the work of God.

Offering is a mystery. It is a physical thing that manifest in the spiritual. Every offering is duplicated in the spirit and it turns into treasures that are stored in the bank of Heaven. Offering and gifts to the work of God are also building materials which are used to build our Heavenly home.

 I heard the story of a woman who had a strange dream. In her dream, she died and was carried by angels to Heaven. On getting to Heaven, she saw great mansions that could not be compared to anything she had ever seen or imagined. She was excited as she was expected to be shown her own mansion. She was attracted to a particular beautiful mansion. The angel told her the mansion belongs to her house maid. She became more excited and expectant. She imagined that if such magnificent mansion could belong to her house maid, that hers would be unimaginable. She patiently waited as the angel continued the tour of Heaven. She then noticed that they were leaving the Porsche part of Heaven to a less attractive part. She was shocked to be told that a shabby looking house was hers. She challenged the angel citing her maid's mansion. She questioned why her maid should have a mansion and she a shack.

To her surprise she was told that heaven only build with what you give to the work of God on earth. Her maid was a regular tither, giver to the poor and supporter of the work of God but she herself hardly did any of the above without complaining. What you sow is what you will reap.

The proper analysis of Philippians 4:15-19 clearly reveals a secret about giving and building treasures in Heaven. Let us read the whole of the scripture for clarity.

Philippians 4:15-19 *"Now ye Philippians know also, that in the beginning of the gospel, when I departed from Macedonia, no church communicated with me as concerning giving and receiving, but ye only. For even in Thessalonica ye sent once and again unto my necessity. Not because I desire a gift: but I desire fruit that may abound to your account. But I have all, and abound: I am full, having received of Epaphroditus the things which were sent from you, an odour of a sweet smell, a sacrifice acceptable, wellpleasing to God. But my God shall supply all your need according to his riches in glory by Christ Jesus"*.

Paul was talking about the mystery of giving to the work of God or to the needs of the ministers of God. The Philippians were looking for opportunities to sow into the life of Paul the Apostle. While Paul was in Thessalonica, they sowed several times to meet the needs of Paul. In verse 17, Paul clearly stated that he accepted the gift, not because he desired a gift but that the gift was to be credited to their spiritual accounts.

He called the gift a sacrifice to God with a sweet smelling aroma. Paul was implying that any gift given to the work of God is a direct sacrifice to God Himself.

In verse 19, Paul exposed another mystery and benefits that awaits those who support the work of God. He promised them that God will supply all their needs according to His riches in Christ Jesus.

My conclusion is that every clean and sincere offering or gift we give to the work of God will be recorded and credited to our Heavenly Accounts.

WHAT WILL ENSURE YOU THE KINGDOM OF HEAVEN?

CITIZENSHIP OF HEAVEN:

The first thing that will ensure you the kingdom of Heaven is the acquisition of the **Citizenship of Heaven**. The citizenship of Heaven guarantees you access to entering the kingdom of Heaven. The citizenship of a country gives you leave to enter the said country except you are denied by the revoking of your nationality.

God has so made it that the only means to having the citizenship of Heaven is to accept the covenant of the death of Christ on the cross. One must accept and confess this sacrifice which declares Christ as Lord and Saviour. This confession comes with a scriptural mystery. The mystery is that the moment a person makes the confession and believes it in his or her heart, the spirit of the person is immediately recreated and a new man is born. Once this is done in the spirit, the individual is given the right of son-ship and citizenship of Heaven. It is now left for the person through the reading of the word to come to the knowledge of his or her rights and the use of such rights and privilege.

"That if thou shalt confess with thy mouth the Lord Jesus, and shalt believe in thine heart that God hath raised him from the dead, thou shalt be saved. "Romans" 10:9

The bible further asserts that:

"Except a man is born again, he cannot see the kingdom of God" period. John 3:3

"For God so loved the world that he gave his only begotten son, that whosoever believeth in him should not perish but have eternal life." John 3:16

This must be the first step to Heaven. There is no other way to acquiring the citizenship of Heaven and entering Heaven. Your membership of a church or how good you are is not enough to grant you access to Heaven.

The above explanations cannot be fathomed by human reasoning. It is a faith thing.

Act 4:12 Salvation is found in no one else, for there is no other name under heaven given to mankind by which we must be saved.

John 14:6 Jesus saith unto him, I am the way, the truth, and the life: no man cometh unto the Father, but by me

2. ENDURE TO THE END

The book of Revelation emphasised the need to endure to the end. Why endure to the end? Endure what?

The Bible tells us that the path to Heaven is a narrow one and few are they that find it. It is a road full of afflictions and requires us to carry our cross and follow Jesus (The Way).

There is this false teaching that once you have accepted Jesus, that you are guaranteed Heaven. This is a delusion. It only gives you access to see and experience the kingdom of God on earth and opens the opportunity to enter heaven. Entering is solely your responsibility through the grace that has been made available. You must enter by faith through the help of the Holy Spirit. You must endure, you must keep away from sin and do not live in sin. If you sin, you must quickly confess and repent. If you pleasure in your sins, there is no guarantee that you will make it to Heaven.

One thing is worth noting. God enables you to endure by His spirit. He makes available all you need to prevail but you must do the prevailing else God would be seen as partial.

The Israelites were delivered from Egypt and were set on their way to the promise land. Not all got to the Promised Land but they that obeyed and endured.

We must be ready to get into Heaven at all cost. We must not just accept Jesus alone, we must be ready to endure and enter; for narrow is the way. It is like a man who has a passport and visa to travel back home but refuses to go to the airport to get a ticket. If such a man stays put, he will never be able to board a plane and will not be able to get home.

Many start well in their journey to Heaven. They accept Christ and remain fervent running the race till they meet fierce resistance from the devil. Some give in at this stage. Some even deny Christ and dump their citizenship of Heaven. They no longer see the Heavenly race as a worthwhile race.

The parable of the sower in Luke 8:13 best explains it.

"They on the rock are they, which, when they hear, receive the word with joy; and these have no root, which for a while believe, and in time of temptation fall away".

Temptation is a must and we must learn how to deal with temptation by the word or we would lose out completely.

The journey to Heaven is not butter and bread. The devil will throw everything at you. His hate for you is so strong that he will do all his best to stop you from making Heaven. In return, you have to resist him with all that you have. You have to use all spiritual weapons at your disposal to resist him. The good news is that God has given you all the provisions to resist the devil.

Why is the devil so mad at your attempt to make it to Heaven? The answer is simple. He was kicked out of Heaven and knows the beauty of Heaven. You were created to take his place in Heaven. To add salt to his injury, you were given the power to become a son of God. This mystery is hard for Satan to accept. That man can be called a son of God.

"But as many as received him, to them gave He power to become the sons of God, even to them that believe on his name:" John 1:12.

Satan is determined to stop you at all cost. You must be determined to resist him and make Heaven at all cost. Expect him to attack you even in church but do not quit and do not take offence.

3. OBEDIENCE

God is big on loyalty and obedience. Nothing drives away his presence like disobedience without repentance. Obedience attracts him. Satan was chased out of Heaven because of disobedience. Disobedience can rob you of Heaven. The disobedient cannot make it to Heaven. Do not deceive yourself that you love God and that you are a child of God therefore can make Heaven while still walking and living in sin.

Mathew 7:21 *Not everyone that saith unto me, Lord, Lord, shall enter into the kingdom of heaven; but he that doeth the will of my Father which is in heaven*

The passage above is self-explanatory. It is not all those who say father, father that make it to Heaven but those who do the will of the father. Do everything you can to obey the word of God and leave the rest for God to sort out.

The mystery about the Love of God is that if you are willing, He will for sure give you a helping hand by his spirit. Obedience activates God's favor. The acts of obedience so captivates God that He would make you a promise and seal it with an oath.

The obedience of Abraham to the call to sacrifice his only son so touched God that he swore to bless him. It is that blessing that the nation of Israel is still enjoying till date. Christ was also a consequence of the blessing of Abraham which we are all enjoying today.

In these last days, God has given us an instruction on the only path to Heaven. He has made it clear that there is no other way to Heaven except through Jesus Christ. He announced it in scripture. Obeying the instruction of following Christ as the way to Heaven is the instruction God has given. Those who believe Him by faith prove to Him that they obey Him and He has gladly made Heaven available to them. Refusing to accept Jesus is like making God a liar and it grieves Him.

"He that believeth on the Son of God hath the witness in himself: he that believeth not God hath made him a liar; because he believeth not the record that God gave of his Son." 1 John 5:10

Conclusively, to make Heaven, one has to be steadfast in obedience. Get rid of anything that will cause you to disobey the word of God. The

Bible explained this when it recommended that we cut off our hand if it will lead us to hell.

"And if thy right hand offends thee, cut it off, and cast it from thee: for it is profitable for thee that one of thy members should perish, and not that thy whole body should be cast into hell." Matthew 5:30

What it is simply saying is that, nothing is worth giving in exchange for Heaven. It is better to lose everything on earth and make it to Heaven than to gain or keep the things on earth and lose Heaven. The things of this earth will someday pass away but Heaven is for ever and ever. It may sound foolish to you but it is the truth.

God uses the foolish things to confound the wise. If you have never thought of Heaven, begin to think of it now.

4. Forgiveness

Apart from accepting Christ, one major command, which for sure, guarantees your salvation, is forgiveness. This seems to be the most difficult thing for most people to accept in a world that is so full of hurt and wickedness; a world where men sit down and plot evil and carry them out without remorse. When they finish their evil acts, sometimes they ask you to forgive them only when they have been caught or put in a corner.

Forgiveness is not an easy thing. How do you forgive a man who intentionally destroyed all your life labour? How do you forgive a man who lied about you and sends you to life in jail? How do you forgive a man who raped you and still mocked you in court? How do you forgive a person that killed your family and let you to rot?

It is difficult yet God expects us to forgive as a precondition to entering Heaven. If you do not forgive, your sins will also not be forgiven. Entering heaven is really a costly affair yet it is attainable.

Mathew 6:14 *For if you forgive other people when they sin against you, your heavenly Father will also forgive you.*

The logic is this, you too have offended God. You have insulted Him, you have robbed Him, you have done everything unimaginable to him even without knowing it, yet He is willing to forgive you. He is waiting for you to ask for forgiveness. The moment you ask for forgiveness, He forgives you without going through your sins or records.

God expects us to do the same. The question is how? He can easily forgive because He is God but we are flesh. How do we manage? The pain is too deep. How does one forgive?

God expects us to come to Him and receive the grace to forgive. He proved it in His son Jesus Christ.

Jesus had been falsely accused, beaten beyond recognition, sentenced to death and made to carry His cross. He was ruthlessly nailed to the cross. In the midst of the pain, He had the wisdom to look unto God the father for strength to ask for forgiveness for those that were about to put Him to death.

"Then said Jesus, Father, forgive them; for they know not what they do. And they parted his raiment, and cast lots." Luke 23:34

Jesus knew the principles of making it to Heaven. He knew He must forgive in order for Him to make it to Heaven because at that time he was in the flesh. If it was mandatory for Jesus to forgive in order to return to Heaven, who are we not to forgive? God is not a respecter of any man. If He says forgive, then you must forgive.

 You might be a good Christian and a good person but if you do not forgive, you will not enter the kingdom of Heaven.

You have trusted your husband or wife and they have cheated on you. You are so hurt that you have sworn never to forgive. Please try and let it go. It is not worth missing Heaven for anything. If swallowing your pride, shame and pain is what it will take to make heaven, then let it be so.

I have sworn to myself that I will never miss Heaven over any person, situation or circumstance. I will let it go and let God be the judge.

As a pastor, I have sown my life into people and they just walk away. Some walk away without saying farewell, others walk away sticking a knife in your back. Some walk away destroying your name. Some refuse to walk away but remain to tear down your work, after which they go rejoicing, yet God commands that we let go in order not to miss heaven.

If anyone is meant to be bitter, I could be the most justified but I can't afford to miss heaven so I just let go.

I read and listen to the testimony of one pastor Ikechukwu from Nigeria who claimed to have died and came back to life after some days. I believed his testimony because there were lots of witnesses to testify to that. One striking thing in his testimony was that at the end of his experience of Heaven and Hell, the angel frankly told him that if the chapter of his life was to close, that he would have had his place in Hell.

Pastor Ikechukwu could not believe his ears. As far as he was concerned, he was a good man. He had accepted Jesus Christ; he was a faithful pastor and husband. What was his error?

A day before he had an accident and died, his wife had slapped him on his face. To an African husband, especially an Ibo of eastern Nigeria, that was a great insult. He was so bitter that he refused to forgive her. She tried to appeal for forgiveness but he was too hurt to talk to her. That simple act of unforgiveness disqualified him for Heaven. He was given another chance to return to earth to share his testimony.

Do not compromise Heaven with unforgiveness. Make it at all cost. There is no price too big to pay.

Heaven at all cost. What is your take?

You do not just pray to go to heaven. You simply take action.

The first action is to accept Jesus as your Lord and personal savior.

You can do that by confessing this simple fact into your life.

WHAT YOU MUST WATCH OUT FOR

Of all the signs pointing to the end, there are a few that we must all watch out for. Why watch out for these ones specifically? It is because these are the ones that can stop you from entering heaven if you fall to them. Matthew Chapter 24 verses 9-13 are too strategic. The truth is that they are happening right now and many especially in the church have ignored it.

9, 'then shall they deliver you to be afflicted, and shall kill you: and ye shall be hated of all nations for my name's sake.

10, and then shall many be offended, and shall betray one another, and shall hate one another.

11, Many false prophets shall arise, and shall deceive many

12, and because iniquity shall abound, the love of many shall wax cold.

13, but he that shall endure unto the end, the same shall be saved.

In our present age, Christians are like endangered species. In the west, they will prefer you talk about yoga, and any religion than talk about Christianity. The moment you mention the name of Christ, people get offended. Sometimes, they get visibly offended and it reflects in their change of color. Christians are been killed everywhere in the world and nobody gives a damn about it. If somebody from other religion dies, it makes headline and immediately investigations are set in motion. This is the mark we must bear for our Lord; to be hated by all nations.

It has become clear that many false prophets have arisen with great signs and wonders. The weak are easily led astray.

Iniquity within and outside the church has become so common that so many people prefer to keep away from church. In the process, they lose their faith and salvation. Iniquity has increased the rate of falling away from the faith. Many Christians have been abused and defrauded so much that they do not trust anything that has to do with God.

The truth here is that we must take the above warnings serious and expect these things to happen. We must focus on God and do not judge God by the behaviour of a Christian. We are all flesh. God is God and man is man. Do not let your love for God grow cold because of the activities of other Christians. These abnormalities in the body of Christ are Satan's game plan to discourage you and cause you to abandon your heavenly race. You must be determined to make heaven at all cost irrespective of what presents itself.

The key word here is endurance. In enduring, we must endure to the end. Only those who endure to the end will make it to heaven. Do not be among those that will fall away. Hold on to your faith and heaven will be attained at all cost.

If you want to start your journey to heaven by first accepting Jesus Christ into your life, please repeat this prayer and believe it in your heart and you will become a new creature and on your way to heaven.

"God I know I am a sinner and that your son Jesus Christ came to die for me. I accept Him as my Lord and personal savior. I repent of all my sins. Wash me with the blood of Jesus and forgive me for all my sins. Write my name in the book of life. Thank you for accepting me and saving my soul in Jesus name."

Having said the above prayers, a miracle has taken place in your life. You are now a child of God and a citizen of heaven.

Find a church where the bible is truly preached and start walking with God in obedience by the power of the Holy Spirit in Jesus name.

See you in heaven.

About The Author

Mike Chuks Nwanegbo is a pastor in the Redeemed Christian Church of God. He is presently the Coordinator of RCCG Belgium Mission. He is a graduate of University of Port-Harcourt and an ex-student of the Continental Theology Seminal Brussels. He is a Pastor, teacher of the Word, motivational speaker, and recording artist.
Mike Chuks Nwanegbo believes in moving people to Godly excellence with a focus on making heaven at all costs.
He is married to Pastor (Mrs) Boma Nwanegbo and they are blessed with three lovely children; Gloria, Praise and Redeemed.